Additional Public
by Victor Kweg

Beyond The Passion:

What It Takes To Achieve Success In Business

(Pathway to Business Success Series)

by Victor Kwegyir

Pitch Your Business Like A Pro:

Mastering The Art Of Winning Investor Support For Business

Success

(Pathway to Business Success Series)

by Victor Kwegyir

The Business You Can Start:

Spotting The Greatest Opportunities In The

Economic Downturn

(Pathway to Business Success Series)

by Victor Kwegyir

You've Been Fired! Now What?

Seize The Opportunity, Creatively

Turn It Into A Successful Reality

by Tonia Askins and Victor Kwegyir

QUOTABLE QUOTES FOR BUSINESS

Lessons for Success

Victor Kwegyir – MSc

International Business Consultant, Coach, Mentor & Speaker

QUOTABLE QUOTES FOR BUSINESS

Published by VicCor Wealth Publishing
www.vikebusinessservices.com

First Edition
ISBN: 0956770665
ISBN-13: 978-0-9567706-6-0
ISBN-13: 978-0-9567706-9-1 (E-book)

PATHWAY TO BUSINESS SUCCESS SERIES

Printed in the United Kingdom
and the United States of America

Cover and interior design: Vanessa Mendozzi

To request Victor for speaking engagements,
interviews, mentoring, proposal writing, ghost writing and publishing, coaching or consultation
services, please send an email to:
victor@vikebusinessservices.com

Victor's books are available at special discounts when purchased in bulk for promotions or as donations for educational and training purposes.

Limit of Liability/Disclaimer of Warranty

Dedication

I dedicate this book to all entrepreneurs and business owners committed to delivering quality products, excellent services and creating wealth for their generation.

Acknowledgments

I am grateful to everyone who has been there for this journey and to everyone who has inspired me with their encouragement and helped me to put this fifth publication together, another exciting resource for entrepreneurs, business owners and aspiring entrepreneurs.

I am always grateful to God for continued mercies, strength, wisdom and ability to do what I do; to my pastor, Pastor Matthew Ashimolowo, President and Senior Pastor of Kingsway International Christian Centre (KICC), for continued inspiration to strive for excellence and explore possibilities to make an impact in our generation; to all my great friends and family who have been a great network of support to me in my journey; Michael Ajose, Mrs. Kemba Agard, to Mrs Frances Mills on your special memorable landmark celebration, to Pastor Ade D'Almeida – KICC, and to my entire family for their prayers, encouragement and support. You have all contributed in many ways to make this a reality. I appreciate you. THANK YOU all once again!!!

Contents

INTRODUCTION

You can never be short of lessons after working in a field for over twenty years, inspiring, challenging, motivating, equipping, and coaching others to establish and grow successful businesses. The lessons learned along the way and the desire to continually see others succeed is the reason for my constant sharing of quotes, principles and anecdotes on social media platforms and blogs.

As has been said, success is the culmination of various factors. It is also said that 'success starts in the mind'. What is shared in this book is intended to help shape your thinking as you navigate through business.

It is my hope that this collection of principles, quotes and lessons can be used as a refresher manual for business owners or business minded people, to stimulate their minds and enable them to stay on course and remain relevant in business.

The journey to success in business has never been a straightforward road. Irrespective of how smart you are, you can be caught up in the routine of daily operations and never make the break to the next level without taking time to feed your mind, engage it and task it to think differently and do better.

The compilation of these lessons is intended to offer you, as an entrepreneur, business owner or aspiring entrepreneur, time tested lessons that inspire you daily on your journey to greater success.

A

ABILITY

1.

Believe it or not, we are all created equal but with varying abilities. It is how much we invest in ourselves and our abilities that determines how we are received.

ACCOMPLISHMENT

2.

The desire for accomplishment in life is a sure indication you've been blessed with the core elements necessary to make it happen.

3.

I have heard it said that 'if it will be, it will be.' However, I say to you 'if it will be, it will depend on you working with God.

ACHIEVEMENTS

4.

Until you believe it you can't imagine it, until you imagine it you can't see it, and until you see it you can't possess it.

5.

'Doing' is always a better option than just 'trying' because doing gets you more focused and there is no room to give up, whereas trying hands you the choice to give up anytime.

6.

More is accomplished in life by a person who is guided by principles than by one who relies on their will. When your will fails let your principles prevail because you stand a better chance of making success of your dream.

7.

It is the battles you choose to fight and win that determines how much you can accomplish and how far you can go in this life.

ADVERTISING

8.

Advertising may be the only way customers form their first impressions of your business well before they ever buy from you

9.

An advertising strategy must support your marketing strategy. The aim is to attract the customer, capture his or her attention and leave an impression and some level of curiosity.

10.

You advertise to introduce your product or service but the quality of your product and the value it delivers to the customer is what brings the returns.

ATTITUDE

11.

Attitude is a silent force that can make all the difference between success and failure.

12.

Attitude counts in business. Courtesy, respect for time, addressing people by their name or appropriate title, use of sorry, please and thank you can significantly impact your bottom-line. Never throw them to the wind as a business owner.

13.

I have heard it said before that, "what you don't know cannot destroy you". I disagree with that. Because in business, what you don't know and your competitors know, can be fatal to your survival and success.

B

BOOTSTRAPPING

14.

What sets bootstrapping apart from other forms of business funding is that it relies heavily on entrepreneurs' frugal thinking, creativity, thriftiness, planning and cost-cutting efficiency skills.

BUSINESS

15.

There is a difference between a hobby and a business. Define which one yours is and make it stand out.

16.

Just as the common saying, 'do not put the cart before the horse' says, do not enter a business without good understanding of how it works.

17.

In business, your best is not enough without adequate knowledge of the industry, right strategies, expert advice and smart actions.

18.

A business has a right to exist and profit from its operations, as long as it continues to solve customers' problems, stays relevant and offers sufficient value.

19.

Establish your identity, be bold and clear in what you are delivering, either as a business for profit, a charity or social enterprise. The customer has too much on their mind to keep wondering.

20.

For every established business there is a story behind its success or continued existence.

21.

Nothing stays static in life, at least not in this fast paced 21st century business environment.

22.

Complexities in business are best managed by simple rules and principles that serve as pointers in the process of elimination and clarification.

23.

In business someone or something has to introduce you to your next level of promotion, platform and breakthrough. The question is, what will they/it say about you and your abilities?

24.

To be a trendsetter is much better and rewarding than a trend follower, both in life and in business.

BUSINESS GROWTH

25.

For a more sustainable business growth strategy it is better to bring down cost than increase prices. Because that always gives you more room to improve efficiency and increase productivity.

BUSINESS IDEAS

26.

No matter how great your idea, it's not a business until you build it into one.

27.

A business idea can spring from one's passion. However, to run a successful operation a significant number of other skills and factors must be in place.

28.

It is not enough to fall in love with an idea and pursue it. It is critical to always put it to the 'economic viability test' first.

29.

The best source of business ideas is a gap in the market. Look for it and start a business that provides a new product or service to fill it or improve on an existing product or service.

30.

The easiest way to come up with a business idea is to look for a problem to solve. And if it matches up with your passion, skill set or experience, that is even better.

31.

Business ideas are like human reproduction – they never cease to be birthed as long as there is constant interaction between the brain and questions of life.

32.

If you believe in your idea and are willing to work smart and hard at it, sooner or later things will fall into place. You have to start it first though.

Check out '31 Ways To Spot Business opportunities' from my book — THE BUSINESS YOU CAN START! Available on Amazon, Kindle, iBookstore, Barnes and Nobles, and bookstores worldwide.

BUSINESS MODEL

33.

A business model that creates the right kind of products or services, and potentially makes the lives of customers better, can easily attract the right investment towards a successful existence.

BRAIN

34.

Until you consciously employ the brain it will go to sleep on you. You must feed it, challenge it and use it. That is the way to get it fully engaged in life.

BRAND

35.

Until you become a household name, presentation always counts. Never allow anyone to convince you otherwise, or discount the importance of your presentation.

36.

Your brand must differentiate you from what your competitors are offering. Until then you do not stand the chance of competing effectively.

37.

If branding is a process, then it stands to reason that there must be a point where the process is initiated. The question is, at what point do you start the process to set yourself apart?

38.

Building a brand is like building a city. A city has a network of components such as roads, houses, libraries, and shopping centers, so does a brand.

39.

Consistency, both visually and verbally, is the key to creating a strategic brand.

40.

No one is better than the other person, except that some make the effort to package themselves well. And that, ladies and gentlemen, makes a whole lot of difference.

C

CHALLENGES

41.

The thing about challenges in life is that, what one person looks at and cries "Obstacle! Problem! Impossible!" another shouts "Opportunity! Potential! Advantage!". It all comes down to perspective. Failing to see this has cost many so much.

COACHING

42.

Your business coach is not your best buddy, but the next best pair of eyes to help you see through the maze and make right decisions without emotional attachment.

43.

A coachable spirit or attitude is essential for your success as an entrepreneur. Without it, you are better-of not signing up to any business coaching package or hiring the services of a coach.

Do you need a proven Business Coach with a passion for your success? Sign up to my one-on-one Comprehensive Business Coaching package, designed to help you work smarter, improve results and enjoy doing it for maximum success. Whether you are now seeking for business opportunities, starting a new business or an existing business owner seeking to improve results significantly, I am glad to help you. To get started email: victor@vikebusinessservices.com now!

COMPETITION

44.

To thrive as a business you have to outshine your previous standard by developing a rich portfolio of skills, services and products that puts distance between you and the competition.

45.

In business your advantage over the competition is largely dependent on what you know and do that the competition does not know or practice, which ultimately sets your brand apart.

46.

The more choices customers have the more creative a business must become to compete effectively.

47.

Competitive advantage is a 'must have' to succeed in business. If it is not in your products, it must be in the way you deliver your service. It enables customers and clients to clearly see the difference and easily choose you above the rest.

48.

The most challenging of all business strategies is competing for the customers' attention to spend their hard earned cash on your business.

49.

To compete only on price is not always the smartest strategy, especially in the long term because it can affect your margins significantly.

COMPLAINING

50.

To complain only makes you keep dwelling on the problem without freeing the mind to think through potential solutions. Be wise. Free the mind to generate the solution you require.

51.

Achievers, successful people and change agents 'get on with it'. Laziness, on the other hand, causes people to become expert moaners and complainers.

CONFIDENCE

52.

Having confidence in the wrong thing is as bad as having no confidence at all.

53.

By all means be confident. It is necessary for life and business success. It can open doors and get great deals struck, help you to take bold steps, and even gain a great following and influence. But please, don't be confident in ignorance, it only diminishes your value and exposes you to ridicule.

CUSTOMERS

54.

As a business you've got to come to terms with the fact that not everyone is your target client or customer.

55.

A smart business makes every effort to see the world through its customer's eyes, enabling it to better understand and serve them.

56.

Never over-promise and under-deliver in business. It has never been a clever strategy if you are in business for the long haul.

57.

It has been said that "the greatest part of any organization is its employees". I will stress, that the most important person in your business when you start is you, and the most important person to your business is your customer.

58.

To deliver excellent customer experience, be knowledgeable about your product and deliver it with excellence, while being flexible and making it obvious to your customers that your operation is run to suit them and not to suit your own convenience.

59.

It costs much less to secure repeat business than to sign up a new customer. Never forget that.

60.

Clients and customers often tend to treat you based on how they see you do business. Do not compromise on conducting yourself professionally.

61.

Successful business people are customer-focussed, not product-focussed. You must do everything you can to adapt to changing times and customer needs over the lifetime of your business.

62.

Successful businesses know who their customers are, understand their needs, and know how to reach out and interact with them.

63.

It is better to see the customer as 'doing you a favour' by choosing you above the competition and patronizing your products and services rather than the other way around.

64.

Every contact your customers have with you and your business is an opportunity for you to cement a lasting reputation with them.

65.

Creating customer value must be a key element in any business offering. One of the smartest ways to win customers involves a basic understanding of how to create an offering that customers value more than what the competition is offering.

CREATIVITY

66.

The mind's ability to be effectively creative is at its full function when consistently focused on one goal.

D

DECISIONS

67.

Making a decision opens your eyes to a great number of
possibilities which otherwise would have seemed non-existence
when your attention was not focused.

DELEGATION

68.

Delegation allows you and your management team to focus on
your primary functions.

69.

To effectively delegate aspects of your business or process you
must choose the right person with the right skills, motivation
and interest in the success of the task and business.

DISCIPLINE

70.

Discipline, like integrity is a great asset in business. However, it can only work for you when you practice and live by it consistently.

DISTINCTION

71.

Everyone has got something that distinguishes them from everyone else, if only they can identify it, develop it, polish it up and package it right.

DREAMS

72.

People who make things happen are driven by their vision and dreams and not by the help they can get from others or the availability of the right conditions and support. Because often, they have to make the things happen. That is what makes them achievers.

73.

Keep dreaming, but you've got to wake up to make it happen.

74.

Expectations breathe hope and energy into the pursuit of a dream. It is an essential driving force without which there will be nothing to strive for. Have an expectation for your future.

75.

A dream is frustrated when one keeps setting unachievable goals. Break the cycle and set realistic goals.

76.

Dreams are realized by doing. Some dreams require just enough to ensure a movement forward. Others require great strength and power applied over days, weeks, months, years and decades.

77.

There is always something to do and a defined step to take to start the process in realizing a dream. The question is, do you know what to do and where to start to kick-start the process?

78.

Taking action is the proof of your belief in your dream. And the more you do it (practice), the better you get (improve skill), and the better the results (proof of progress).

79.

If the dream is important, you will be less concerned about the price you have to pay to get the right advice, to do research and plan for its successful execution.

E

ECONOMIC DOWNTURN

80.

Economic downturns are among the most notorious periods for the birthing of great ideas, you just need to adjust your perspective.

81.

Both downturn periods and boom time periods are an ideal time to step out because both can support the argument for starting a business.

ENTREPRENEURS

82.

An entrepreneur is a person who originates an idea then goes on to initiate and navigate the processes necessary to get a business started.

83.

A real entrepreneur makes things happen, even in the face of imperfect conditions and limited support.

84.

Entrepreneurs are not job seekers. Real entrepreneurs are job creators.

85.

Entrepreneurs who master the art of pitching, easily attract the support they need.

EMPLOYEES

86.

When your recruitment criteria and objectives are flawed,
they reflect on the dedication and commitment of your
employees.

87.

Going to the labour market with a cheap mentality rather
than a skills and attitude mind set positions you to attract poor
quality, lesser skilled motivated employees.

EXCELLENCE

88.

Excellence has no limits because there is always room for improvement.

89.

It stands to reason that when you enjoy what you do, it fuels your quest to become better at it, and to deliver excellence.

90.

If you are going to deliver then do it with excellence because that is the only way to guarantee repeat business.

91.

In business what your connections cannot do for you, your diligence and excellence will secure for you.

92.

Aim for excellence and you shall not be disappointed.

EXCUSES

93.

Excuses are easy to find. It is not a surprise that it is not deemed an achievement to be the one to always come up with one.

F

FAILURE

94.

Sometimes, even with the best of information, advice and resources, you may fail but this cannot scare you from doing nothing. Even in failure there are great lessons to be learned for a better tomorrow.

95.

Don't exaggerate the size of the potential failure so that it paralyses you from stepping up and stepping forward.

96.

Most businesses fail, not because of the 'big picture' but because of the little things that were given less attention or completely ignored.

97.

Refusing to manage one's expectation of the time it takes to attain success in business is one of the major causes of business failures within the first 2-3 years.

98.

An entrepreneur or business owner's failure to manage their finances is the single most important factor that can sink the business.

99.

Failure is an indication you have tried, potentially learnt from your mistakes and are ready to try again.

FEEDBACK

100.

Feedback is one of the quickest routes to innovation. And it costs almost nothing because customers are often generous with it.

FREEDOM

101.

Freedom comes with two caveats: responsibilities if you exercise it and consequences if you abuse it.

FUNDING

102.

All business funding options have their pros and cons. Never sign up to any without full understanding of what you are getting and what you are giving away.

103.

Funding should not be the first consideration when weighing up options for becoming an entrepreneur or starting a business. Rather, the first steps to undertake on the way to realizing business dreams are usually research, seeking expert professional advice and then using all of this information to begin planning.

104.

Funding is never a problem. It's the solid logical case of providing a credible solution to an existing problem that guarantees a good ROI (Return On Investment) for the investing community that matters.

G

GOALS

105.

If the rewards of achieving your goals are not greater than your fear of moving towards them, you won't have enough willpower to propel you to step up and step out to make them happen.

106.

Defining clearly the 'why' of your goals sets you up with the right basis to build on for greater success.

GREATNESS

107.

Greatness is not in your title, but the result of the impact you made in life.

108.

The uniqueness of great people tends to make them look abnormal to the ordinary person.

GROWTH

109.

Being satisfied with too little is an enemy to growth and expansion.

110.

Your distinction in business is as important as the quality of products and services you deliver. It is the way to sustain consistent and successful growth.

H

HEADLINE

111.

The headlines mean nothing without the background story.

HELP

112.

Seeking help as a business owner is part of the journey. Ensure you get help from the right sources, network with the right people and seek advice from the right experts. It will make a significant difference to your 'bottom-line'.

I

IGNORANCE

113.

Ignorance is like getting lost in the crowd, yet being too arrogant to ask for help. It is the greatest killer of mankind. Never make friends with it, and don't be boastful about it.

114.

A business succeeds by what it knows and not by what it is ignorant about.

INNOVATION

115.

Until you are inspired by something, innovation means nothing to you.

116.

Innovators ask the questions 'What if …?', 'Why not …?', 'When can …?', 'How can …?', And they don't stop there but move a step further to seek ways to answer the questions.

117.

Innovation starts with seeing change as an opportunity, not a threat.

118.

Innovation does not have to mean a dramatic change in the business. Instead, it could start by simply tweaking processes to save cost and time or adopting simple new but more effective strategies towards greater profitability and growth.

119.

At the heart of every innovative process is the question, 'why can't …'?

INVENTION

120.

Every invention is precipitated by the question, Why can't?, Why not?, How about?, And of course the 'chance discoveries' that pop up every now and then from an original research focus.

121.

You can invent a thing but not a business because business is meant to be developed over time.

INVESTORS

122.

Your average investor is smarter than you think. Focus on building a solid case that makes you and your business attractive and you will win them over.

123.

At the end of the day a typical investor would just like to know how their money will help your business and how they will earn profit from their investment.

K

KNOWLEDGE

124.

The right knowledge gives you confidence and informs you of the best options available to you.

L

LIFE

125.

Life has many circles. You are either propped up to dream
and see beyond your

immediate circle or you are weighed down so you can't lift up

your head above your immediate circles.

M

MARKETING

126.

Never rely on family and friends as the target for your business market research. Extend your research to others in your network, and anyone you can find, even complete strangers and naysayers, and avoid one sided feedback.

127.

Effective marketing is registering in the customer's mind that you are not easily replaceable.

128.

A value for money promotion strategy is not just dependent on advertising on any available platform but a platform available to and accessed by the target customer. A successful advertising campaign strategy aims at the best combination of the two.

129.

Your marketing strategy can only benefit your business strategy … if you use it.

MIND

130.

The mind is an excellent breeding ground for everything you sow and permit to grow.

131.

The human mind is unbelievably rich with great ideas and possibilities. Employ it, feed it, challenge it, and it will work wonders for you.

132.

The mind-set of an entrepreneur is as important as the business idea itself and the success of the business is directly linked to it.

133.

Having the right mind-set for business is simply non-negotiable because it is the foundation to everything else you will have to do to run a successful business.

134.

Success at anything starts in the mind. Just don't let it end as a beautiful image of what it could be. Work at it to bring the imagery into reality.

MONEY

135.

It is said that 'money makes the world go round'. If that is the case, then get yours and enjoy the ride.

136.

A business must have a clear, unique, and well-understood vision or purpose and it must be much broader than just making money from your passion if it wants to thrive.

N

NEGOTIATION

137.

Having a mind-set that everything is negotiable in business is key to your success.

138.

In negotiations it's not about winning or losing, it's about all parties feeling they received something of value when the deal is struck.

139.

In negotiating a job you never provide a quote when you don't have enough information. Ask questions and get all the necessary facts and figures to better cost the work.

140.

A successful negotiation is achieved when you make allowances for things that may mean little to you while giving something to the other party that means a lot to them.

141.

A good negotiator is able to decipher between what is said, written or not said, and what is meant.

142.

Negotiation can be learned and the skill can be improved on over time and with practice.

O

OPPORTUNITIES

143.

Some opportunities only come by once in a lifetime, so seize them. Make sure not to miss them. If you do, just wipe your tears away and move on. You still have a life to lead.

144.

To benefit from opportunities you must always be in the 'prepared mode'. It is the best way to position yourself to take advantage of opportunities when they come by, often unannounced.

145.

Opportunities in business are not always given, they are taken. That is simply the fact. Better get used to it.

146.

Obstacles often birth opportunities for those who choose to look at them differently.

147.

Obstacles and opportunities are more closely related than often thought. There are always opportunities to be explored, even at the point of your greatest obstacles.

148.

Not every opportunity is for you. That is the reality of life. Stay focused and don't get distracted with everything that looks like one.

149.

When a person is hungry to make a difference they are often less bothered about how opportunities are presented to them.

150.

Rewarding opportunities are often sought out like a hunter consciously goes in search of prey.

151.

Where there is a void, there is an opportunity. Find it and meet the need. Where there is no need for something, create one. This is how businesses are created and ideas flow.

152.

Every business opportunity looks, feels and appears as a problem to someone. The people who choose to look at a problem with a different mindset, are the ones who will keep increasing their economic power.

153.

An opportunity to prepare for anything in life is a luxury you cannot afford to lose. Unfortunately it almost always comes unannounced.

154.

Every business opportunity has a risk element to it. You can allow it to cripple you from pursuing it, or take it up as a challenge to cover all the basis as much as you can, so that the risk becomes a calculated risk.

ORDER

155.

Create order and you will find great beauty and substance in what you do.

P

PARTNERSHIP

156.

Never partner with anyone in business who does not take responsibility for their actions, see the need to be accountable, or is not driven by the same values or going in the same direction as you.

157.

It is not a smart business proposition to enter into a partnership with someone focused solely on personal ambition and self-promotion and not on the partnership.

158.

It is very important to be honest and upfront with the friends and family you ask to help fund your business.

159.

An important cautionary note in business: money has a way of destroying even the most beautiful friendships and relationships. You certainly don't want that to happen to you and your close associates. Always draw up an agreement beforehand!!!

PASSION

160.

Passion is an important starting point in identifying business opportunities as well as running a successful business operation.

161.

No matter how passionate you are about your idea and business, it is simply impossible to know it all.

162.

The right reasons and a passion to offer solutions to people's problems is the antidote to quitting in business, even in the toughest of times.

163.

If you are passionate about what you do work is not a struggle. Or course, there may be challenges, but the work itself is a joy.

164.

Passion is a necessary driving force to get you through to the other side when a business faces challenges and falls on hard times.

165.

Passion evokes confidence in you to drive the business.

166.

Passion enables your customers to feel the vibe and buy into what you are offering.

167.

It is naïve to believe in 'following your passion' without managing your expectations along the way.

168.

Passion is necessary in driving the entrepreneur or business owner on the journey to success.

169.

Passion generates energy and excitement for the task ahead.

170.

Unless you are passionate about what you have on offer, you may not get anyone to want to pay for it, let alone survive economically.

171.

Passion is just one piece in the puzzle of what it takes to realistically succeed in business.

172.

Your passion positions you for opportunity and opportunity makes way for success

Check out 'How To Follow Your Passion And Make A Success Of It' from my book – BEYOND THE PASSION! Available in paperback and eBook format on Amazon, Kindle, iBookstore, Barnes and Nobles, and bookstores worldwide.

PERSISTENCE

173.

Persistence is a major key to successful living. Until you stop, you have every chance of getting what you desire.

PITCHING

174.

To pitch a business and attract the attention of an investor, the investor has to be sold on YOU, YOUR IDEA and YOUR VISION.

175.

Clarity, confidence, and good communication skills enable you to pitch you, your business and your vision right.

176.

Passion is a major factor in pitching to investors and winning them over to support you, your business and your vision.

177.

It is important to note that whereas you can be woefully and inadequately prepared for a pitch, you can never be over prepared for it.

178.

When pitching to investors, you can have all the facts and details to hand but if you are not able to 'paint the kind of picture' that will leave a lasting and positive impression on the audience you will fail.

179.

To deliver a successful pitch you must align your body language and your content and seek to establish a relationship of trust as quickly as possible through the way you communicate with your audience.

180.

The elevator pitch should leave your listeners interested, impressed and eager to hear more. It must push the right buttons, fuel the interest of the investor audience and give you a foot in the door.

181.

Ultimately an effective sales pitch must present the product or service features, accessibility, and benefits to the prospect.

182.

Every entrepreneur, whether naturally gifted or not, will need to develop and master the art of pitching, because one way or the other it is the one skill that will be called on throughout the life of a business.

183.

In a sales pitch, the conversation must ultimately enable you to uncover the prospect's needs, understand these needs, and show them that what you are selling can help them meet that need, fix the problem or help them accomplish what they are trying to accomplish.

Check out 'Six Steps On The Art of Masterclass Pitching' from my book – PITCH YOUR BUSINESS LIKE A PRO! Available in paperback and eBook format on Amazon, Kindle, iBookstore, Barnes and Nobles, and bookstores worldwide.

PLANNING

184.

The level of commitment, and the value a person places on the planning of the business, says a lot about how far they are likely to go and how successful they can become.

185.

Planning offers a glimpse into the future. Action crystallizes and brings your dream to life. And the right strategies delivers success to you.

186.

Plan for your success. Don't just dream about it.

187.

Focusing on limitations instead of creating a plan first will rob you of the enthusiasm and drive necessary to start your dream business.

188.

Nothing happens just because you wish it to happen. Planning before stepping out is non-negotiable.

189.

Your executable plan is the future you create today.

190.

Create a plan and be willing to change the plan if you don't succeed at the first try. It is the best way to bounce back and make a success of your journey.

191.

When you choose priorities over urgencies, you stop reacting to circumstances and start creating a life of purpose, enabling you to plan and spend time on that which significantly makes your tomorrow better.

192.

Nothing can be accomplished without praying, planning and preparation.

193.

A good plan should help you clearly articulate the why; the what; the how; and the when to take the right actions to fulfil your dream.

PROBLEMS

194.

Every business solves a problem. It provides a solution to the problems of yesterday, of today, or of tomorrow. The question is, what problem is your business solving?

195.

To be in the 'problem solving' business positions a start-up business to survive the failure curve much better than others. Of course, this is made much better with the adoption of the right strategies and networks.

196.

Always seek to understand the problem at hand before jumping at it. Having a better understanding of a situation, gives you an edge over the search for the right solution.

197.

Business is about solving problems. Once you get that you are on course for greater success.

198.

Never allow problems to ruffle you – they are opportunities in disguise.

199.

Every problem is an opportunity to become better, to know better and to do better.

200.

The mark of a successful businessman or woman is how they deal with and overcome obstacles.

PRODUCT

201.

Every product you sell has a service element to it. Neglecting it can lead to losing the entire business. Be smart and give it equal attention.

PROGRESS

202.

The truth is that, if you don't have a target, you can't measure progress. If you don't have a plan, you can't set a target. And if you don't measure your progress, you have no basis to improve.

PURPOSE

203.

Knowing your purpose in life gives you focus. Focus means less distraction. Less distraction brings you an increase in productivity. Increased productivity translates to success.

Q

QUALITY

204.

Quality trumps shoddiness in business. It evokes good value to the returning customer.

205.

When the quality of your work hushes even your toughest critics, you are on course to the heights of true excellence.

R

REPUTATION

206.

Good reputation is necessary for business success. A good reputation comes from higher service standards, quality products, consistency in delivery, and availability to the customer.

207.

A smart business owner strives for a good reputation, works for it, astutely maintains it and improves on it at every opportunity.

RESEARCH

208.

In business ignoring the research is not smart. It can be suicidal to disregard what the available research is suggesting.

209.

Doing research, seeking expert advice and using what you learn to create a plan are the first steps to realizing business dreams.

RESILIENCE

210.

When you go into business with a partial resolve to succeed,
it is easy to throw in the towel at the least challenge. An
unflinching resolve with the right reasons will always spur you
on, even in the toughest of times.

RESPECT

211.

Respect is earned by conducting yourself responsibly and
acting maturely, not the other way round.

RESULT

212.

If you want results bad enough, you would do whatever it takes to get it done without compromising your delivery.

RISK

213.

To succeed in business, you must be prepared for the risks and challenges that come with it.

S

SALES

214.

A good sales strategy is only as good as the importance you and your employees attach to it and how well understood it is by them.

SHORTCUTS

215.

Shortcuts for quick gains have never been a good strategy for lasting business success. If in doubt, check out the bad press and record fines imposed on businesses that fall foul of such strategies.

216.

Shortcuts don't often stand the test of time.

217.

Short-sightedness (in thinking) is a major characteristic of non-achievement in life and business. It is very important to always have an eye on the long run

SOCIAL MEDIA

218.

Getting your network, subscribers and visitors to engage, and consistency in what works best for your business, are keys to the success of any social media strategy.

219.

Social media is like a puppy that needs attention and like a beast that needs feeding with the right food at the right time to work for you.

220.

Using social media has become the online version of word-of-mouth marketing. Do not ignore the social etiquette, learn to be sociable and make it work for you.

SOLUTIONS

221.

Solution providers often command more value than problem makers.

222.

It is not a legitimate business if it does not solve a problem or meet a genuine need.

STANDARDS

223.

The standard is never too high for the one going places.

START-UPS

224.

Start-ups take off because the founders make them take off. There may be a few that took off, grew organically and caught up with the market right from the onset but usually it takes some sort of push and effort to get them going.

225.

Never start a business just because there is available support to help you as an entrepreneur, but because there is a problem you can solve and enough customers willing to pay economic price for the solution.

STRATEGY

226.

In business, unless you have a carefully crafted business strategy, you are simply operating by trial and error.

227.

A well-crafted business strategy helps you to articulate the direction a business will pursue and the steps it will take to achieve these goals.

228.

A good strategy defines the nature, direction and value system of the business as an entity.

229.

A well-crafted business strategy with the right implementation plan can make a huge difference in an organization's quest to grow and to become more profitable and successful.

SUCCESS

230.

Successful business people make time for events, strategies and activities that matters to their profitability and growth.

231.

Successful businesses don't just happen. There is always sweat, great sacrifices, good decisions, right strategy choices and smart work practices employed behind the scenes.

232.

Your success rate in any project or assignment in life is dependent on how much you know and how much preparation you invested in before setting off.

233.

Run the business as a business and you shall see true profits, increase and success. Run it like a charity and you shall only gain handouts.

234.

No amount of natural skills or talent is enough to earn you sustained success without nurturing, consistent training and perfecting of such skills and abilities. It is the only way to guarantee you stay at the top of your game.

235.

Your motivation to succeed may be strong, but your motivation not to fail should inspire you to be smart and strategic in your business.

236.

Every industry has its secrets. There are the obvious and easily accessible secrets and there are the less obvious ones. Those who succeed in business explore and exploit the obvious ones and constantly seek out the less obvious via expert advice, quality resources platforms and training. The question is, do you have a grasp on what makes your kind of business succeed?

237.

One of the greatest challenges for most people in life is knowing the difference between what is good and what is right, at any given time. Settle that and you are on course to navigating your way to a successful life and business.

238.

An important success principle in business is in understanding you, your customers, your business, your industry and environment and employing the right strategies with deliberate effort to make it work.

239.

Time invested, strategic effort, discipline, systems, structures and knowledge offer the best shot at business success.

240.

Success in business requires adopting time-tested ways of analyzing situations, processing available information and making right judgement.

241.

The abilities and gifts you do not possess are often exactly what will not bring you to your place of fulfilment and destiny. It is the ones you possess which, when perfected, will bring you your greatest achievements and success. Redirect your frustrations towards perfecting them.

242.

To succeed in business, you need help. However, you need to acknowledge you need it.

243.

Measuring success by how much profit you make can be misleading.

244.

The desire to succeed is not a guarantee to becoming successful. Choices, not circumstances, are what determine success.

245.

The pathway to the heights of success requires a significant amount of investment of your time and money. You can only be a smart investor in this journey when you put value on what matters to your success above what makes you look or feel good in the short term.

246.

Successful people make time for people, activities and events that matter to their journey.

247.

Success is not attained by chance but a product of consistent and persistent action in the direction of your vision, with a significant amount of passion.

248.

Success can come in different forms and levels but the principles behind it are one and the same.

249.

Good foundations are prerequisites for lasting success.

250.

The desire to succeed is not a guarantee of becoming successful. It is the steps and
actions you take that guarantee success.

SYSTEMS AND STRUCTURES

251.

Systems and structures are the pillars for growth and expansion in business.

252.

When you create the right structures and systems in your business you give God the platform to bring you increase. Because structures and systems allows for order and God works by order and not chaos.

T

THINKING

253.

It is impossible to profit from natural talents, without employing strategic business thinking and investing techniques.

254.

The 4 T's of life – Think Things Through Thoroughly.

255.

To master business is to master the way successful business people think.

TIME

256.

Productivity is a function of time. Managing your time gives you a better chance of becoming productive.

257.

Consistency and time are your best bet in business.

258.

The best time to start your business is to assess your readiness, know when you are ready based on your personal circumstances, vision and preparation.

259.

It's not how much time, but what you do in the time that makes it meaningful to all parties.

260.

True success is a product of strategic effort over a period of TIME. Time is therefore a friend to make good success of your business dreams

261.

True success eludes those who have less appreciation of the value of time.

TRUST

262.

In business you've got to make your word count. Even if you agreed to offer something for FREE. Because it is not about the offer, it is about the promise - Your Word. Because TRUST is built on honoring your Word every time you promise.

V

VALUE

263.

Value is a 'gold mine'. There is almost no limit to how much you can tap in, to distinguishing your business from the pack.

264.

People often pay for what they value most. That said, an individual or community who does not like to pay for something of value, simply do not value it and never benefit from it.

265.

Placing value before price is much cleverer than the other way round. Never compromise on that.

266.

Value and price are not the same. However, good value has every potential to command good price.

267.

Value gives a business more options to carve out a niche for itself.

Assessing the worth of your product or service on the basis of value proves to be much more wholesome than using the cost or price of the item.

VISION

269.

People driven by vision beyond their immediate need are more able to survive the 'now' pain and willing to sacrifice for a better tomorrow.

270.

People who make things happen are driven by their vision and dreams, and not by the help they can get or the availability of the right conditions and support. Because often, they have to make the things happen and that is what makes them achievers.

271.

Having a bigger vision also enables you to 'stick with it' and to continue to work at it to find better ways of delivering your products and services until you get the right profitable balance.

272.

Vision, Purpose, Dreams, Goals are all great. However, if you don't believe in them and take steps to make them happen, they just remain as words with no relevance.

W

WEALTH

273.

Wealth creation is not an event, it is a process. Smart people plan for it, and don't just wish it.

WISDOM

274.

Wisdom dictates that you focus on doing things right rather than doing them fast. After getting the fundamentals right, you can always build on them, and run with them to a successful completion.

275.

When you have nothing to say, it is better to keep your mouth shut. You will look more dignified than saying something stupid, which you may regret and never have the chance to take back.

WORK

276.

To work hard involves exerting much physical energy and being busy. To work smarter involves taking advantage of quality information and advice, strategies and tools, and using them to execute a given task on time. Choose to be a smart worker. It yields better and lasting results than hard work.

CONCLUSION

What I've shared with you in the above pages is the result of being in business for the past two decades. I have used these quotes in my coaching and mentoring sessions with many clients over the years, hugely impacting their mind-set and perception of what works in business, as well as the basic principles and strategy tips that can inspire success.

With the feedback I receive daily on my postings on social media, as well as from my previous publications, I am confident these simple quotes, principles and lessons will make a significant impact on your journey to success in your business and life as whole.

Check out my other publications on the next few pages, read them and share your thoughts by way of reviews. For one-on-one coaching, please don't hesitate to send me an email victor@vikebusinessservices and we can get started. Look forward to working with you to achieve greater success in life and in business.

ABOUT THE AUTHOR

Victor Kwegyir is an international business coach and mentor, consultant, entrepreneur and the founder and CEO of Vike Invest Ltd, a growing International Business Consultancy firm in London, UK. He is also the founder of Executive Ghost Writing and Publishing Service.

He has over twenty years' experience in business, and holds a Master's in International Financial Systems.

Victor is a motivational speaker who has challenged and equipped people with the knowledge and practical tools in starting and growing successful businesses through his presentations at international conferences and seminars.

Victor is also a regular guest speaker and contributor to entrepreneurial development and business growth & profitability radio shows with over 80 guest appearances under his belt. He has his own blog and contributes to other blogs and business finance and management platforms, such as LinkedIn, StartUS Europe and other websites around the world.

In addition to this book, Victor is the author of:

- *"Beyond The Passion - What It Takes To Achieve Success In Business"*
- *"Pitch Your Business Like A Pro – Mastering The Art Of Winning*

Investor Support For Business Success"

- *"The Business You Can Start – Spotting The Greatest Opportunities In The Economic Downturn"*
- *"You've Been Fired! Now What? - Seize The Opportunity, Creatively Turn It Into A Successful Reality"* (coauthor)

These titles are available on Amazon, Kindle, ITunes, iBookstore, Nooks, Sony Reader - eBook edition, Barnes and Nobles, Vikebusinessservices.com and book stores near you.

To request Victor for one-on-one business coaching, mentoring and consultation services, speaking engagements, ghost writing services and interviews please send an email to victor@vikebusinessservices.com.

Victor's books are available at special discounts when purchased in bulk for promotions as well as for educational or fund raising activities.

IT IS MY EXPECTATION THE LESSONS, PRINCIPLES AND STRATEGIES SHARED FROM MY 20 YEARS EXPERIENCE IN BUSINESS WILL INSPIRE YOU TO KEEP YOURSELF AND YOUR BUSINESS AHEAD OF THE COMPETITION AS YOU REACH FOR GREATER SUCCESS IN YOUR BUSINESS. DON'T HESITATE TO CONTACT ME IF YOU NEED HELP NURTURING YOUR PASSION, STARTING A NEW BUSINESS, EXPLORING THE POSSIBILITIES OF EXPANDING YOUR EXISTING BUSINESS. OR JUST IN NEED OF A PROVEN COACH TO HELP YOU NAVIGATE THE BUSINESS JOURNEY MORE PRODUCTIVELY AND SUCCESSFULLY, IN YOUR QUEST TO IMPROVE RESULTS AND BUILD A THRIVING BUSINESS.